An Account of Winfield Manor in Derbyshire

WINFIELD MANOR.

AN ACCOUNT OF

𝔚infield 𝔐anor

𝔍n 𝔇erbyshire,

BY

SIDNEY OLDALL ADDY, M.A.,

AND

JAMES CROSTON, F.S.A.,

WITH AN

INTRODUCTION BY RICHARD KEENE.

ILLUSTRATED WITH PLATINOTYPES AND
ENGRAVINGS ON WOOD.

DERBY:
PRINTED AND PUBLISHED BY RICHARD KEENE,
OPPOSITE ALL SAINTS' CHURCH.

SUBSCRIBERS.

His Grace the Duke of Devonshire, K.G., Devonshire House,
Piccadilly, London (2 copies.)

Henry Allpass, F.R.S.L., for Devonshire Library, Derby.

Miss Askey, St. Mary's Gate, Derby.

Charles H. Bakewell, Quarndon, Derby.

Benjamin Bagshawe, Sharrow, Sheffield.

George Bailey, 32, Crompton Street, Derby.

H. H. Bemrose, J.P. (6 copies).

Thomas Booth, Post Office, Nottingham Road, Derby.

Charles Bowring, Park Grange Derby.

S. E. Bourne (Mrs.), Holbrook, Derby.

W. H. Bramley, 23, Roe Street, Derby.

Geo. Brigden, Iron Gate, Derby.

Benjamin Brindley, The Crescent, Vernon Street, Derby.

Benjamin Bryan, 1, Victoria Street, London, S.W.

A. Buchanan, J.P., 8, Wilson Street, Derby.

Arthur Cates, 7, Whitehall Yard, London, S.W.

W. Clarke, Wood Brook, Loughborough.

Ed. Clulow, Jun., Derby (6 copies).

Geo. Clulow, 51, Belsize Avenue, Hampstead, N.W.

Andreas Edward Cokayne, Bakewell, Derbyshire (3 copies).

Richard Geo. Coke, Brimington Hall, near Chesterfield.

Colonel E. T. Coke, Debdale Hall, Mansfield.

Edwin Cooling, Mile Ash, Darley Abbey (2 copies).

M. A. Cooper (Mrs.), Rowsley.

W. E. Cooke, 6, North Parade, Derby.

C. W. Cooke, Spondon.

Henry Cupit, George Hotel, Alfreton.

N. C. Curzon, J.P., Lockington Hall, Derby.

Jno. Dean, Sadler Gate, Derby.

William Downing, Olton, near Birmingham.

T. W. Evans, M.P., Allestree Hall, Derby.

Robert Evans, South Road, The Park, Nottingham.

Samuel Evans, 5, Iron Gate, Derby.

Thomas Evans, Pen-y-Bryn, Derby.

G. R. Faire, The Limes, Barkby, Leicestershire.

W. D. Fane, Melbourne Hall, Derby.

Richard Fawcett, Wirksworth.

Edwd. Fisher, Abbotsbury, Newton Abbot.

William Fletcher, St. James' Street, Derby.

S. Gilbert, 50, Queen Street, Derby.

C. H. Goodwin, 115, Friar Gate, Derby.

William Gouk, Mansfield, Notts.

William S. Greaves, Ironville, Alfreton.

L. J. Greensmith, Longcliffe House, Charnwood Street, Derby

Geo. Cressy Hall, J.P., Swanwick Grange, Alfreton.

Fred. J. Harte, 3, Clifton Square, Lytham.

A. Seale Haslam, North Lees, Derby.

Edwin Haslam, S. Helen's Street, Derby.

W. G. Haslam, North Street, Derby.

Henry Headland, Derwent Street, Derby.

H. W. Hollis, Butterley Hall, Alfreton.

E. Horne, Market Place, Derby.

W. Howe, Matlock Bath.

E. N. Huggins, Albert Street, Derby.

Mrs. Hunt, 1, Winfield Terrace, Chester Road, Old Traf
Manchester.

Samuel Hunt, Wingfield, Ashton-on-Mersey, near Manchester.

John Hunter, Field Head House, Belper.

John Hunter, Jun., Matlock Road, Belper.

Thomas Hurst, Free Public Library, Surrey Street, Sheffield.

John Jackson, Stubbin Edge, Ashover (2 copies).

W. Wynne Jeudwine, Chesterfield.

J. Jones, 14, Market Place, Derby.

Rev. Charles Kerry, Morton, Alfreton.

Charles E. Keyser, M.A., F.S.A., Merry Hill House, Bu
Watford.

A. Geo. Kirby, Grove House, Wavertree, Liverpool.

J. D. Leader, F.S.A., Broomhall Park, Sheffield.

Thomas Lee, South Winfield.

Hy. Litherland, Derby Crown Porcelain Works.

Alexander Macpherson, 13, S. Mary's Gate, Derby.

W. Mallalieu, Swallows' Rest, Ockbrook.

W. J. McDonald, 14, St. James' Street, Derby.

Edwd. McInnes, 100, Osmaston Road, Derby.

Miss Moseley, Friar Gate, Derby.

Thomas Haden Oakes, J.P., Riddings House, Alfreton (4 copi

James Peach, 10, St. Alkmund's, Derby.

R. Kyrke Penson, F.S.A., Dinham House, Ludlow.

Miss Popple, Castle Donington.

Samuel Rickman, Walton Cottage, Chesterfield.

J. B. Robinson, 15, Derwent Street, Derby.

Fred. J. Robinson, 45, Friar Gate, Derby.

Charles Rosson, Uttoxeter New Road, Derby.

S. Rowbottom and Son, Alfreton (4 copies).

Subscribers.

W. Hy. Sale, The Uplands, Derby.

T. Sharratt, Green Lane, Derby.

T. G. Sheldon, J.P., The Square, Congleton.

Miss Sowter, St. Peter's Street, Derby.

Geo. E. Statham, Matlock Bridge.

George Sutherland, Arboretum Square, Derby.

Alfred Swingler, Douglas House, Derby.

William Taylor, (Warden), Winfield Manor Ruins.

John Turner, 14, Victoria Street, Derby.

W. Wake, Osgathorpe House, Sheffield.

John Walker, Uttoxeter Old Road, Derby.

T. E. Walmsley, Sadler Gate, Derby.

Jno. Ward, 36, Normanton Street, Derby.

Wm. Harvey Whiston, Derby.

Wilkins and Ellis, 12, St. Peter's Street, Derby.

R. Wildgoose, The Poplars, Holloway, near Cromford (3 copies).

James Wilson, 35, Bull Street, Birmingham (2 copies).

Charles Winter, Hornsey, London, N.

ILLUSTRATIONS.

follows this Introduction. If this is not a correct view, where was the cellarage? He has proved that large quantities of wine were consumed here, and his view is still further strengthened by the fact of a spiral staircase leading to the crypt from the dais of the banqueting hall. Mr. Croston seems in doubt, but thinks it may have been a store or guard-room; while the Rev. Dr. Cox and others look upon it as a retainers' hall, similar in fact to the servant's hall of the present day, and which frequently in large houses is situated beneath the great hall or banqueting-room, as at Kedleston, Newstead, and Alton Towers. If it was used as a retainers' hall, it must have been a very dark and cheerless one, more especially when its three small windows opened into the "cloister" which once ran on the north side to the chapel. But there is as great uncertainty in naming this a cloister as in calling the undercroft a crypt—it was most probably a later addition with a flat roof. It seems then that the conclusions of Mr. Addy are more than probable; but there will always be difference of opinion respecting this mysterious vaulted room which has *four* entrances and *no* fireplace. The stone paving has been removed, and the rain filters through from the grassy floor of the roofless banqueting hall and makes dark pools in the mud below, hastening the work of destruction. The beautiful masonry of the vaulting-ribs with their ornamented bosses at the intersections are noted and admired by all, but most writers like most visitors overlook the eight rudely-carved keystones of the wall-ribs, six of which are depicted in Mr. Ferrey's most truthful series of drawings. They are invisible in the gloom, but can be seen by striking a match.

One represents a mask with leaves issuing from the eyes and mouth, others are of angels with scrolls or musical instruments. One of the latter is given in the following tail-piece.

Another mystery about this old ruin may be noticed. How was it supplied with water? At the present day all the water used by the tenant farmer has to be fetched from some distance in the water-cart usually seen standing in the porch. It is said there was a well in the outer court which fell in many years since; and a late tenant of the farm, Mr. Cupit, speaks of lead piping having been found in the fields to the south, leading, it is supposed, from Fritchley, some two miles distant, from whence the water could be conveyed. The supposition that this "dignified combination of castle and mansion" was so supplied is supported by the fact that a field there is called "Conduit Field" to this day.

Other riddles will present themselves to the thoughtful observer as he examines the ruined walls and studies the architectural details and interpolations of this most beautiful and interesting place; knocked about as it has been by Cromwell's cannon balls, then repaired and altered to suit the requirements of its new owner,* and finally used as a quarry from which was built the ugly house below. It is gratifying to find his later descendants and the present

---

* In 1678 Winfield Manor was conveyed to Immanuel Halton, the astronomer and mathematician, and it was during his life that many alterations were made to render the shattered place fit for his abode. The Banqueting Hall seems to have been the principal part he inhabited, which was divided into two storeys and also by a wall

in Wright's Vocabularies) *cellarium* is defined as "incleofa ; *sic dictum quia in ea colligantur ministeria mensarum vel quae necessaria victui supersunt.*" It thus appears that the cellar was then the place where the various articles necessary to set forth the table were kept. In a pictorial glossary of the 15th century (Wright's Voc.) the names of the various parts of a great house are collected and set out together, but here nothing is said about a retainers' hall, though the pantry, buttery, and spence are mentioned. The "undercroft" at Winfield was the spence. Here the wine, spices, fruit, dishes, &c., were kept by an officer of the household called the spencer, who in monastic houses was called the cellarer. In a very rare and valuable book in the writer's possession, Huloet's *Abcedarium*, 1552, occurs "cellar or storehouse, *cella*," and "cellarer, or he that kepeth the storehouse, *cellarius.*"

Winfield unquestionably means "gorse field." *Win*, meaning gorse or furze, occurs, under various spellings, in nearly all the old glossaries. Moreover it is still in use as a dialectal word in Derbyshire. There is a Winacre Wood near Dronfield.

CARVED STONEWORK OVER THE GATEWAY TO INNER QUADRANGLE.

WINFIELD MANOR.

E may say of Winfield Manor Place* as was once said of a famous city, that it is "bitterly historical." We need only glance for a moment at its ruins to see that the hand of Time has done little towards the spoliation of a house which in earlier days was magnificent, and is now but a sad image of its former self. Its walls are straight and strong, and the wind and rain of centuries have hardly yet effaced the marks of the mason's chisel. The roofless hall, the broken tracery, the obliterated chapel, the marks of cannon shot on the walls—these tell of human passions and prejudices which, all

go down a stone staircase to the cellar,* a large vaulted
and dark room, lying beneath the hall. Here my lord
keeps good store of Sack and Malmsey and many other
rare foreign wines. And there was need that he should

THE CELLAR.

keep a plentiful supply in his cellars, for Ralph Sadler
has told us that the Queen of Scots and her train consumed about ten tuns of wine, that is about two thousand

---

* Several writers, and notably Mr. Leader (*Mary Queen of Scots*,
p. 54), have spoken of this room as a crypt or undercroft, which,
in the broad acceptation of these words, it was. But I think we
may here include in the generic term crypt the specific term cellar.
The ceiling of this room was formerly plastered, and probably white-
washed as modern cellars are. The steps leading to the high table
in the hall are a proof of its having been the cellar.

five hundred and twenty gallons, in a single year. He has also told us that there were two hundred and ten gentlemen, yeomen, and officers living in the house, fifty of whom were soldiers staying there to guard the Queen. These soldiers, he says, had their meat and drink found, and some allowance for wages. The Queen had four good coach-horses which were kept at Lord Shrewsbury's expense, from which we may gather that she sometimes rode out to take the air. And besides all these the Queen had five gentlemen, fourteen servitors, two married women servants, and ten girls and children, making together forty-eight persons. She had fifteen rooms allotted to her in the house. Two of these she used herself, two were occupied by the two married women servants and their husbands, three by the maid servants, and the remaining eight by the gentlemen and officers of her train and the men servants. The Queen's two Secretaries, the Master of the Household, and Dr. Prean had each of them a chamber of his own. The Queen had no furniture of her own, except a few bed hangings and an old chair or two which were much worn. Sadler has also told us that on both fish and flesh days she had sixteen courses at dinner, more or less. Besides these, the Secretaries, the Master of the Household, the Physician, and Dr. Prean had seven or eight dishes, and always dined in the Queen's presence. Wheat was twenty shillings a quarter, a good ox cost four pounds, and sheep were seven pounds a score. Pit-coal was plentiful in the neighbourhood, and was usually burned at the Manor.

But, reader, we will, if you please, say good bye to Mr. Bentall, and turn over an earlier page of history. We will pass from the year 1584 to the time of Henry VI., who reigned from 1422 to 1461 A.D. In this reign we have it on the authority of Camden* that Lord Cromwell, Treasurer of England, built this house, and it was therefore more than two centuries old when the Scottish queen was first a captive within its walls.

The Winfield property had been acquired by the marriage of Sir Ralph Cromwell with Avicia Bellars or Bellairs. The Cromwells were a family of great antiquity in Nottinghamshire, and derived their name from a place called Crumbwell, or Cromwell, in that county. Lord Cromwell, who built this house, married Margaret, sister and co-heiress of William Lord D'Eyncourt. In 1433 he was made Treasurer of the Exchequer during the pleasure of Henry VI., and three years later he was retained to serve the King in the relief of Calais with one knight, twelve men-at-arms, and one hundred and seventy-five archers. In the same year he was made Master of the Hounds and Falcons. Three years later still we find him engaged in a work of piety, namely, in making the church of Tattershall in Lincolnshire, where he had large possessions, a collegiate church. He built the great brick tower there, which is still known by his name. Probably his office of Treasurer brought him wealth by which he was enabled to build extensively. He was Steward and Keeper of the King's Forest of Sherwood, in Nottinghamshire. He died on the 4th of January, 1455, without issue, and was buried in the church of Tattershall, which he had endowed so

* Camden says it was built by *Henry* Lord Cromwell, *temp.* Henry VI. But this is clearly a mistake.

richly. Over his body was placed this inscription in
Latin :—

"Here lieth the noble Lord Radulph Cromwell, Knight, Lord
of Cromwell, formerly Treasurer of England, and founder of this
college, with Margaret his illustrious wife, the daughter and one of
the heiresses of the Lord D'Eyncourt, which Ralph died on the
4th of Jan. A.D. 1455. And the said Margaret on the 15th day of
Sep., 1454. Whose souls God pardon. Amen."

By his will, made the year before he died, he had appointed
no less than three thousand masses to be said for the
repose of his soul. Thus did the Treasurer of England
and builder of the stately house of Winfield die in the
odour of sanctity. As we have seen, he left no children,
and not long afterwards the Manor passed by purchase
of the reversion to the Talbots, Earls of Shrewsbury.

Before we leave Winfield we will cast a rapid glance
upon its later history. In the time of Charles I. it was
held for the Parliament by the Earl of Pembroke, and in
1643 it was taken by the Royalists after a desperate re-
sistance. It was, however, recaptured by the Roundheads,
when artillery was directed against the house from Pent-
ridge Common. Cannon balls are still picked up about
the ruins.

The last scene of our brief tale closes on Immanuel
Halton, who purchased the Manor in 1678 from the then
Duke of Norfolk, and to whose descendant, Halton
Tristram, Esq., it now belongs. Immanuel Halton was a
man of studious and retiring habits. In the great pile of
venerable buildings which he had bought, he pursued, as
his epitaph tells us, the studies of music, mathematics, and
astronomy. From the watch-towers of the Cromwells we

may fancy him, on dark autumn evenings, surveying the spangled heavens. But for him, as for nearly all the men of his generation, the graces of a forgotten art had no charm. He did not hesitate to make this picturesque abode conform to the tastes of the age in which he lived. It is, however, comforting to reflect that the men of his day knew nothing of those feeble forgeries which we call "restorations." They showed their own individuality. And thus Immanuel Halton, who was both gentleman and scholar, did not scruple to alter this picturesque ruin in order to make himself a convenient dwelling-house. For this purpose the great hall formed a suitable site, as witness the windows in the north side. But it was left for a later generation of the Halton family to make a quarry of the Manor, when they built their house in the valley.

APPENDIX.

THE unusually spacious cellar at Winfield suggests that much wine must have been drunk in England about the time when this house was built. That such was the case we have the amplest evidence. When Edward IV. in 1473 was about to make a progress through Norfolk we find John Paston writing to his brother "to warn William Gregory and his fellows to purvey them of wine enough," for, he said, "every man beareth me in hand that the town shall be drank dry as York was when the king was there."* Dr. Whitaker in his *History of Craven* gives some copious extracts from a compotus of the Canons of Bolton, in Yorkshire, of which he makes an analysis. He computes that the prior and canons of that house consumed about 1,800 gallons of wine each year, and he considers that the full complement of that monastery consisted of about two hundred persons. This amount is not large for so splendid and wealthy a monastery, and it contrasts somewhat favourably with the quantity consumed by the Scottish Queen and her suite

---

* *Paston Letters.*

at a later period.   The Queen herself, however, used wine
for "bathing" as well as drinking, as appears from the
following letter* sent by the Earl of Shrewsbury to the
Marquis of Winchester and Sir Walter Mildmay :—

It may please you to understand, that whereas I have had a certain
allowance of wine, amongst other noble men, for expenses in my
household, without impost, the charges daily that I do now sustain,
and have done all this year past, well known by reason of the Queen
of Scots, are so great therein as I am compelled to be now a suitor
unto you, that ye will please to have a friendly consideration upon
the necessity of my large expenses.   Truly two tuns in a month have
not sufficed ordinarily, besides that that is occupied at times for her
bathings, and such like uses; which seeing I cannot by any means
conveniently diminish, mine earnest trust and desire is that ye will
now consider me with such larger proportion in this case as shall seem
good unto your friendly wisdoms, even as I shall think myself much
beholding for the same.   And so I commit you unto God.   From
Tutbury Castle, this 16th of January, 1569.

Your assured friend to my power,

G. SHREWSBURY.

The Queen's health was not good, and it seems probable
that her physicians had prescribed bathing or rubbing the
body with wine.   Instances are not wanting of people
being rubbed with wine, as we rub with camphorated oil
now, and of children being dipped in brandy to strengthen
them, as it was supposed.

In 1575, whilst the Queen was detained in Sheffield
Castle, we find Ralph Barber making a journey from that
town to Rouen and back, to fetch wine, confectionery,
damask, and other articles.   The account furnished by

---

* Lodge's *Illustrations*, ii. 27.

him on his return to Sheffield is here printed,* and it will
be found of interest, not only as illustrating the manners
and customs of the period, but as showing, for our present
purpose, what need there was of ample cellarage both at
Sheffield and Winfield. The monotony of the Queen's
imprisonment was relieved by the little presents which
were sent to her. The year before Barber went to Rouen
we find her expressing a hope that her uncle, the Cardinal
of Guise, will send her a couple of pretty little dogs.
"For," she says, "besides reading and working, I take
pleasure only in all the little animals that I can get."† She
asks for the little dogs to be sent in baskets, very warmly
packed. It will be noticed that the following account is
divided into two parts, the one being the payments made
in France, and the other those made in England.

FRANCE.—*The accompt of me Ralph Barber, for one
voyage made unto Rouen, for your Lordship‡ as
followeth;* 1575.

	£	s.	d.
Imprimis, paid unto Mr. Jasper Dublett for three tuns of French wine, at twelve pounds fourteen shillings the tun	38	2	0
Item, more, unto Peter Deylaport, for eight tuns of French wine at thirteen pounds fourteen shillings the tun	109	12	0
Item, more, for one tun of Orleans wine	15	0	0

* It is printed by *Lodge* (vol. ii., p. 144) with the old spelling
and contractions. These I have modernized, and, where possible,
extended.

† Leader's *Mary Queen of Scots*, p. 345.

‡ George Talbot, Earl of Shrewsbury.

allowed to remain unchallenged, for about the 19th year of the same reign a suit was instituted by Henry Pierpont, Knt., who claimed as heir of the inheritance of Margaret Gra, descended from the family of Heriz; the result was a compromise, by which certain manors were vested in the family of Pierpont, and the manor of Winfield assured to the Lord Cromwell.

Ralph, Lord Cromwell, descended from a family of some antiquity, was summoned to parliament as one of the barons of the realm in 4th Henry IV., he being then only twenty-three years old; in the following reign he attained to considerable power and influence, and was appointed to several offices of honour and emolument, enjoying, as it would seem, in an extraordinary degree, the confidence and favour of the king. In 11th Henry VI. he had granted to him the office of Treasurer of the Exchequer, and three years afterwards he was retained to serve the king in the relief of Calais with one knight, 12 men-at-arms, and 175 archers. In the same year he was made master of the king's hounds and falcons with the wages and fees belonging thereto, and subsequently had conferred upon him for his services a grant of £40 to be received annually during the royal pleasure out of the manor of Whasshynburgh, then in the King's hands. On the first of February, 23rd Henry VI., he had granted to him and his heirs, for the services he had performed to the King, the offices of constable of the King's Castle of Nottingham, and steward and keeper of the Forest of Sherwood, the parks of Beschewode and Clypston, and the woods of Bellow-Birkeland, Rumwode, Ouselande, and Fullwood, in Nottinghamshire. The building of the present manor-house of Winfield was commenced by this Lord Cromwell on the site of a more ancient structure, and completed after his death by John Talbot, Second Earl of Shrewsbury, to whom he had sold the reversionary interest in the manor.

South Winfield continued in the possession of the noble house of Shrewsbury until the death of Gilbert, the Seventh Earl, in 1616, when the inheritance was divided amongst his three daughters and coheiresses, the eldest of whom, Mary, was married to William Herbert, Third Earl of Pembroke, who died in 1630 without surviving issue, when her portion of the estate reverted to Sir William Saville, Bart., father of the First Marquis of Halifax, and grandson of Mary Talbot, daughter of George, Sixth Earl of Shrewsbury by his first wife, Gertrude, daughter of Thomas Manners, first Earl of Rutland. Elizabeth, the second daughter, became the wife of Henry Grey, Earl of Kent, and she also dying issueless, her moiety passed to her uncle, the Eighth Earl of Shrewsbury, whose descendants retained possession of the same until 1709, when Charles, Twelfth Earl of Shrewsbury, by indentures of lease and re-lease, conveyed five-sixths parts of his portion of the manor and estate to Thomas Leacroft, of Wirksworth, the remaining one-sixth part being sold about the same time to Wingfield Halton, Esq. Alathea, the youngest of the three daughters of Gilbert, Earl of Shrewsbury, who claimed, by inheritance, the third portion of the manor of South Winfield, married Thomas, Earl of Arundel, grandson of Thomas, Duke of Norfolk, who was beheaded in 1572, and her grandson, Henry, Duke of Norfolk, conveyed this moiety to his auditor, Imanuel Halton, gentle-

plain and excessively ugly-looking structure on the opposite side of the valley, and all that now remains are the grass-grown courts, the ruined and roofless halls, the crumbling buttresses, the shattered ramparts, and the heaps of hoary ruins on which the everlasting ivy flourishes in all its pride.

The palmy days of Winfield are now .over, and its glory has for ever passed away. Those grey and massive towers—the sad memorials of fallen grandeur, majestic even in decay, and beautiful in their desolation—which once reared their heads aloft and looked down with proud and stern defiance, braving the wintry blast, and rejoicing in the summer sheen, are now crumbling gradually into dust, mocking the vanity of man, and evidencing the impossibility of resisting the silent, yet sure corroding hand of time, which, sooner or later, locks within its desolating grasp the mightiest works of human creation. For—

> "E'en so fares it with the things of earth
> Which seem most constant : there will come the cloud
> That shall enfold them up, and leave their place
> A seat for emptiness."

The situation is exceedingly well chosen. The house stands upon the verge of a rocky knoll which rises boldly from the plain a little to the south of the village, and commands an extensive view over the surrounding country. Its numerous towers, all crenellated and embattled, rising proudly above the spreading woods in which it is embosomed, when viewed from the opposite side of the valley, have a striking and highly picturesque effect, and invest it with an air of grandeur that well accords with the interesting and romantic associations connected with it.

New Works and New Editions.

Lightning Source UK Ltd.
Milton Keynes UK
UKHW020842230822
407709UK00006B/508

9 781379 240983